Successful

Speed-Reading

in a Week

TINA KONSTANT

Hodder & Stoughton

A MEMBER OF THE HODDER HEADLINE GROUP

Very special thanks to Morris Taylor

in the Institute of Management

The Institute of Management (IM) is the leading
organisation for professional management. Its purpose is
to promote the art and science of management in every
sector and at every level, through research, education,
training and development, and representation of
members' views on management issues.

This series is commissioned by IM Enterprises Limited,
a subsidiary of the Institute of Management, providing
commercial services.

Management House,
Cottingham Road,
Corby,
Northants NN17 1TT
Tel: 01536 204222;
Fax: 01536 201651
Website: http://www.inst-mgt.org.uk

Registered in England no 3834492
Registered office: 2 Savoy Court, Strand,
London WC2R 0EZ

Orders: please contact Bookpoint Ltd, 130 Milton Park, Abingdon, Oxon
OX14 4SB.
Telephone: (44) 01235 400414, Fax: (44) 01235 400454. Lines are open from
9.00–6.00, Monday to Saturday, with a 24 hour message answering service.
Email address: orders@bookpoint.co.uk

British Library Cataloguing in Publication Data
A catalogue record for this title is available from The British Library

ISBN 0 340 779985

First published	2000
Impression number	10 9 8 7 6 5 4 3 2
Year	2005 2004 2003 2002 2001

Copyright © 2000 Tina Konstant

Typeset by Fakenham Photosetting Limited, Fakenham, Norfolk.
Printed in Great Britain for Hodder & Stoughton Educational, a division of
Hodder Headline Plc, 338 Euston Road, London NW1 3BH by Cox & Wyman
Ltd, Reading, Berkshire.

C O N T E N T S

Speed-reading is more than simply reading fast; it's about reading smart. Smart reading is determining what it is that you want from any reading material:

1   reading it as efficiently as possible
2   being able to recall information when you need it.

If you master the techniques in this book, you will be able to read and absorb more information in less time than ever before. You might find that you spend less time reading because you manage to get through more information more quickly and the 'I'll get around to it' pile will be less threatening and easier to 'get around to'. Also, when you have learnt how to read non-fiction material faster and more efficiently, you will find that you naturally apply efficient reading techniques to your leisure reading without losing the enjoyment of a good story.

As with anything new, speed-reading takes some practice, but not the type that requires you to put hours aside each day. The aim is to include speed-reading techniques in your daily routine and in doing so become aware of what you read and how you read it. Awareness is the first step to change.

Take just a few minutes each day over the next week and you will learn everything you need to know about speed-reading.

On **Sunday**, you will be introduced to the five-step system – *prepare, preview, passive reading, active reading* and *selective reading* – which will be explained in detail.

On **Monday**, how and why speed-reading works and ways to improve your reading strategy.

INTRODUCTION

Tuesday is an important day – that is when speed-reading and memory techniques are combined.

On **Wednesday**, you will take a close look at how your eyes work while you read. Concentration diminishes when you are uncomfortable or tired. The more you take care of your eyes the better your concentration and consequently your memory will be.

Thursday will be set aside for examining distractions such as internal and external noise, bad lighting and the shortage of time.

On **Friday**, we meet the real world. You will look at how much time you really have to read and how to make the best of it. Sometimes you might only have a few minutes to absorb as much information as you can before having to present ideas on it. We will look at different ways to use the techniques to get as much out of them as possible in the time you have available.

Since it is easy to learn a new technique and then carry on exactly as before, on **Saturday**, you will devise a programme that will help you integrate the new techniques into your daily routine making you a more efficient and productive reader.

The five-step system

Today is your introduction to speed-reading and the first
steps towards effective reading.

- How to use this book
- Speed-reading raises questions
- The five-step system

How to use this book

This book is designed to be a workbook for your speed-
reading skills and a reference for you as you practice.

Each day may be referred to independently. This makes it
easy for you to locate the information you need. Becoming
accustomed to moving freely around a book instead of
reading it from front to back is an important habit to
develop; most authors do not put the information in
precisely the right order to suit *you*.

Which brings us to a most important rule of effective reading:

Make your own reading rules.

A quick guide to reading this book fast and effectively

1 Flick though the book to get a feel for its structure.
2 Read all the boxes at the start of each chapter for an outline of what that chapter contains.
3 Next, read the boxes at the end of each chapter for a summary of each chapter.
4 Finally, start at the beginning to learn the five-step reading system.

As you progress through the book learning new speed-reading skills, practice them on this book. You will find that you get through the book much faster than you would have imagined and you will have had the opportunity to practice your new skill.

Speed-reading raises questions

- What's the fastest possible reading speed?
- How do I remember what I read – when I need to remember it?
- How do I read dry or technical material and maintain concentration?
- Is speed-reading easy to learn?

Firstly, we do not know the limit to the speed at which people can read. The current record holder can read a book the size of *War and Peace* in 20 minutes and answer questions on it!

'Able to answer the questions' is the most relevant part of the exercise. Why spend precious time reading if you do not plan to remember what you wanted to distil from the material? Remembering the information long after you have read it, whether fact or fiction, will be explored on Tuesday.

Speed-reading is easy. The part that needs practice represents only **one fifth** of the reading strategy presented in this book. The rest of the system works simply because you use it.

The five-step system

There are *five stages* to the strategy. By the time you complete them you will have:

- explored the material at least three times
- read what you need to have read

- integrated the new knowledge into what you already know
- acquired an accurate recall of the information
- found the information you require at the time

AND, most importantly, you will have spent a fraction of the time you might otherwise have spent.

To avoid slipping back into old reading habits, accurately follow the five-step process as outlined in this book. Once you are familiar with the system, you can adapt it to any type of reading (articles, newspapers, memos, books or magazines) by combining and omitting steps.

> *The five-step system has one overriding rule:*
> Always know *why* you are reading something.

Whether the reason is 'I want to', 'it looks interesting', or 'because Joe says it'll be a good read' ... doesn't matter, as long as you have one.

The five-step system is:

1 Prepare
2 Preview
3 Passive reading
4 Active reading
5 Selective reading

This system is based on the process of *highlight* and *eliminate*. As you use the system, your aim is to highlight areas for further study and eliminate those that you are certain you do not need.

Depending on how much you want from the book, steps *one* to *four* could take between five and 40 minutes for a book of 300 pages. The time you spend on step *five* depends on how detailed the information you want from the material is.

Steps *one* to *five* will now be precisely detailed. Read through this section once, then, using a non-fiction book you are interested in, try the system out. At this point don't worry about reading fast (as in more 'words per minute') – we'll discuss that tomorrow.

Step 1: Prepare
One reason that reading can be frustrating is due to a lack of focus and concentration. The preparation stage helps you focus on the task.

First:
- Write down what you already know about the subject: key words will be sufficient.

Next:
- Decide what you want from the book: is it general information, enough to write a report on or simply the answer to a specific question?

Always ask yourself these three questions:

1 Why am I reading this in the first place?
2 What do I already know?
3 What do I need to know?

Step 2: Preview
The purpose of previewing a book is to become familiar with its **structure**:

- What does it look like?
- Are there summaries or conclusions?
- it all text?
- Are there any pictures?
- What size is the print?
- Is the text broken up into sections?
- Is it a series of paragraphs?

For a 300-page book, the overview should take about five minutes.

- **Read** the front and back covers, inside flaps, table of contents, index, and scan the bibliography.
- **Determine** the structure of the book; chapter headings, sub-headings, pictures, graphs, cartoons and images.
- **Eliminate** the parts of the book that you are sure you don't need.
- **Highlight** areas you think you do need.
- **Re-affirm** your decision about what you want from the book.

If it becomes clear that the book does not contain what you need, put it away. You will have saved yourself hours of work.

Step 3: Passive reading
Now, you have prepared yourself and you know the structure of the book. Passive reading familiarises you with the **language** in the book. Is it full of jargon? Is the author a *linguafan*? This step works well if you have completed step one (prepare) thoroughly.

A 300-page book should only take between five to ten minutes to passive read.

* Scan the pages at a rate of about a page every few seconds.
* Look for words that stand out and highlight them. They might be names, long or technical words, or words in **bold** or *italics*.
* Study the language: is it technical, non-technical, user-friendly, are you familiar with it?

A MOST IMPORTANT NOTE

If you know **why** you are reading the book you will know **what** you are looking for and words related to your area of interest will stand out. Try this now: look around the room for everything red. Only red. Notice how much and how many shades of red there are in the room. Now, close your eyes and try and remember everything blue in the room ... what did you notice? If you know what you are looking for, you will find it.

Step 4: Active reading
This is the first time you will be doing anything close to reading. Most well-written material will outline the aim or core of each chapter in the first paragraph and the contents of each paragraph will be made clear in the first sentence of that paragraph. So, for more detail:

* read the first paragraph of every chapter; and
* the first sentence of every paragraph.

As you read – cross out, **highlight**, underline, circle, take notes and mind-map. The more thoroughly you do this, the more effective the final stage will be.

Step 5: Selective reading
Here is a thought experiment (don't actually do this unless you want to fall foul of mountain rescue).

Imagine you are to take a trip from London to Edinburgh. You are to use country roads as far as possible. Imagine you have never taken such a trip before, but still you decide not to take a map. On your arrival in Edinburgh, check your time, which will include all the detours you had to take and the stops you had to make to ask for directions. Make the trip a second time with a map, then compare the ease and speed of the two journeys.

The same principle applies to reading. Steps one to four create a map for you to follow. Once you know where you are going and how you are going to get there, the task is much easier to accomplish.

The purpose of the first four steps is to allow you to select what you need or want to read 'intelligently'.

During the first four steps you have decided what it is you want to read, what answers you are looking for and what you are interested in about the subject. You have studied the structure of the book, you are familiar with the language, you have read approximately one third of the content and you have an excellent understanding of what the book contains. You are now in a position to select the sections you really need to read without worrying whether you have missed anything out or not.

To do this most effectively:

- Review the notes you made in step one.
- Add to your notes any information you have gained as you have been reading.
- Ask: 'Do I already have what I have been looking for?'
- If you have what you need, **stop**.
- If not, review the key words you have highlighted in step three and repeat the question: 'Do I have what I want yet?'
- You made notes in step four: review them and again ask whether you have what you want.
- If you decide that you need more information, then go through the book and read the pieces you identified as relevant during the first four steps.
- If you do decide you need to read the entire book you will find you will be able to read it much faster, because, having completed the first four steps, you will know what the book contains and what to expect.

Summary

The five-step system	
Step	**Time**
Step 1: Prepare • Determine exactly what you want from the book. • What is your purpose? • When will you use the information? • Why are you reading?	No longer than five minutes
Step 2: Preview Familiarise yourself with the structure of the book. Go through the book quickly, looking at paragraphs, chapters, cartoons, graphics and general layout.	Approximately five to eight minutes for a book of 300 pages
Step 3: Passive reading Skim to find key words and familiarise yourself with the language. *Your familiarity with the language is a factor determining the speed at which you will be able to read.*	Approximately five to ten minutes
Step 4: Active reading To familiarise yourself with the contents of the book read the first paragraph of each chapter and the first sentence of each paragraph.	Approximately 30 minutes
Step 5: Selective reading Read only what you need to read. Always ask: • Why am I reading this? • When am I going to use the information? • Do I have what I need?	20 minutes at a time

By now, you will be familiar with the layout, language and content of the book, you will have spent approximately 40 minutes with the book and you will have a very good idea of what it contains.

Think carefully again about what *exactly* you want from the material. The length of time you spend on step five depends on how much you decide you need. Whether you want to read it all or just one paragraph on one page in one chapter, it will be an informed decision and you will not have wasted your time.

Now stop reading this.

Think about the five-step system and apply it to the rest of the book.

One of the biggest complaints people have about speed-reading books is that they are too big and take too long to read. Use what you learn, as you learn it, to increase the rate at which you read this book.

DID YOU KNOW?

If you know *nothing* about a subject it is almost impossible to remember what you read. The five-step system helps you build a framework of knowledge, making retention and recall easier.

Speed-reading

It is easier to learn how to do something you have never
done before if you do not have to break old habits to reach
success. Learning to read fast can be challenging because
while you are learning this new improved version of speed-
reading a lifetime of habit is constantly interfering with the
learning process. To develop a secure new habit pattern,
you need to practice.

Speed-reading is not just about reading the words faster
than you did before. Rather, it's about being able to read at
a speed appropriate for the material you are reading. If you
read too slowly your mind will wander, you are likely to
become bored and won't remember anything. If you read
too fast you will reduce the chances of remembering what
you want and will probably become frustrated and stressed
and even less likely to remember.

The more flexible you are with your reading, the faster you
will be able to read and the more information you will retain.

Today will include:

- Factors contributing to speed
- What you need to improve speed
- Increasing your basic reading rate
- Using a pacer
- Different types of pacing
- Skimming and scanning
- 'Getting the message'
- 'It's all in the words' – developing a good vocabulary
- Reading exercises

One way to increase your reading rate and comprehension is to read often. The more you read the better you will become at recognising when you can read fast and when to slow down.

Factors contributing to speed

Factors contributing to the speed at which you can read are:

- **Familiarity with the subject-related terminology** – If you are already familiar with the subject you will already have a framework on which to build and you will be able to read quite quickly because you will not have to stop to think about what the words might mean.
- **Clarity of purpose** – Step one of the five-step system. The clearer your purpose is the faster you will be able to read. Always know why you are reading something.
- **The difficulty of the text** – Some books are just difficult

to read even if you are familiar with the terminology and content – legal writing suffers from this if you are not a lawyer.

- **Urgency and stress levels** – Have you ever noticed that when you absolutely have to read something immediately you find that you can't read it fast? Stress will slow you down. On Tuesday, stress will be considered in conjunction with concentration and memory.
- **Mood** – If you are feeling tired, restless, impatient or irritable, you may find that you will be unable to read as fast as when you are feeling alert, fresh, happy and relaxed. You may not always be alert, fresh, happy and relaxed when you have to read so, if you can, learn how to manage your feelings so that you can concentrate regardless of how you might be feeling at the time.

What you need to improve speed

To improve your reading speed you will need:

- good background knowledge of the subject or, if you do not have that yet, a strategy for building the background knowledge quickly
- familiarity with the language related to the subject
- a good vocabulary
- a desire to learn how to improve your reading
- a good attitude towards reading. Ask yourself the question 'what is that I get from speed-reading?'
- practice – if you can set aside 15 minutes a day for 30

days you will find that the speed at which you can read, the recall, comprehension and the flexibility of your reading will quickly improve.

There are many ways of picking out information at varying speeds. Many people believe that they have to read every word in a book or article. That is only necessary if you have a specific *reason* for reading from cover to cover. Before you decide whether you need to do this *you need to know what information the reading material contains*. Once you have gone through steps one to four, you will be ready to select what you want to read in more depth. Now is the time to **speed-read**. And here is how you do it.

Increasing your basic reading rate

The main reason that we tend to read slowly is because we read with our *ears* instead of with our *eyes* (more about this on Wednesday). The second reason we read slowly is because we are easily distracted by what is on the page and by what is going on around us.

Using a pacer

A pacer is a tool that will help you to eliminate most of your speed-reading problems. A pacer can be your finger, a chopstick, a pencil or pen, anything that you can use to place under the words on the page.

A pacer helps to eliminate most distractions, and it includes an extra sense in the reading process. Using a pacer adds a kinaesthetic, physical dimension to your reading. You are actually *doing* something instead of simply reading. You are involving your hands as well.

Using a pacer helps your reading in several ways.
- It increases your reading rate by encouraging your eyes to focus on more than one word at a time.
- The pacer focuses you on what you are reading instead of allowing your eyes to jump around the page at anything that attracts your attention.

Here is an experiment for you to try. Find someone willing to take part. Ask that person to draw a circle in the air using their eyes. Notice the eye movements – are they smooth or jerky? Do they create a full circle or does it look like they are making corners? Next, ask them to draw a circle in the air with their finger and this time to follow their finger with their eyes. Watch their eyes. Do you notice that the second time their eyes move smoothly, quickly and deliberately?

The pacer also

- helps you move to new lines smoothly and easily
- prevents you losing your place
- prevents sub-vocalisation (the voice inside your head caused by reading with your ears) by speeding up the pace at which you read and allowing you to see more than one word at a time.

How to use a pacer

You can use a pen, a chopstick, a finger, anything you like, as a pacer. To begin, place your pacer on the first word on the line and move it smoothly across the page to the end of the line, then return it to the next line.

Use your pacer to read the next paragraph. Place the pacer on the dotted line and move it smoothly across the line. Re-read the paragraph several times until you feel that you have the rhythm smooth and fast – also, move the pacer just a little bit more quickly than you think you can 'read'.

It is important that the pacer moves smoothly and steadily across the page. If the movement is hesitant your eyes are dictating the pace at which you read and your reading rate will not increase. If the pacer moves smoothly, your eyes, with practice, will learn to keep up and your brain will learn to absorb the meaning of words in a new way.

What was different about reading with a pacer? How did you feel? How much faster did you feel you read? How do you feel about comprehension?

Are you still reading with your pacer?

For the duration of this book read using a pacer. By the time you finish the book you will find that it has become second nature and you will be well on the way to becoming an expert speed-reader.

Different types of pacing

The pacing you are using now is one basic method for guiding your eye across the page. There are different methods of pacing for different types of material and different readers' needs.

Technical material with which you are not familiar
Place the pacer under every line and move it steadily across the page from the beginning to the end of each line. This method ensures that you miss nothing.

Technical material that you are familiar with
Place your pacer under every *second* line. This method encourages you to read more than one line at a time and ultimately to understand the meaning much more quickly.

Material with which you are very familiar
If you are very familiar with the material and you only need to have a general idea about what you are reading you can run the pacer down either the side or the middle of the page.

Ultimately, the more you experiment and the more flexible your reading becomes, the easier you will find it to change from one technique to another.

Practice box – novel exercise

Novels are the best source of practice to develop flexibility in pacing. At the start of the novel you might find that you pace under every line, then as you get familiar with the plot you might pace under every two lines. When the story really gets going and you are looking for the exciting bits in between the description, you might find that you run the pacer down the middle of the page until you find the sections of the book that really carry the story. Your enjoyment of the book is not lessened in any way at all – in fact you might find that you actually finish more novels than you used to.

Hints to increase your speed:

- **Push yourself quite hard**. It is easy to stay in the comfort zone of reading slowly. Once you break through the barrier of believing that you can only remember what you read when you *hear* every word, your enjoyment of reading and your pace will increase.
- **Practice** – often. Use everything you read as a practice medium. Speed-read the instructions on the back of a bottle or the sales blurb on the back of a cereal packet. Instead of just reading as you have previously, read with the **purpose**, ie as fast as you can for good comprehension. Use a pacer when you do so.
- **Build the context first**. The first four steps of the

five-step system will make speed-reading *anything* easy and several times faster than if you were reading it for the first time.

- **The faster you go the less you will vocalise**. Later on today, we will discuss ways of building speed and maintaining it – *play* with these exercises daily until you feel that they are a natural part of your reading strategy.
- **Eliminate or decrease distractions**. On Thursday, we look at different distractions you are likely to encounter and some solutions to them. The more you are able to concentrate, the faster you will be able to read.
- **Read actively**. The techniques you use during step four, you should be using while you speed-read in step five. Take notes, mark and highlight relevant sections, make comments as you read, build reading maps and think about the arguments as you read. If you must do any talking inside your head while you read, choose to make it a debate or dialogue on aspects of the topic with the author. The more actively you read, the better your understanding and long-term comprehension will be.

It is important to remember that:

Speed-reading is not about reading fast all the time. The technical content of the material, the print size, your familiarity with the subject, and, particularly, your *purpose* for reading can affect the speed at which you read. The key to speed-reading is having the *choice* to read as fast or as slow as you wish.

Skimming and scanning

- What are they and what is the difference?
- When to use them?

The difference between skimming and scanning is that when you scan for information you stop once you have it. With skimming you don't stop, unless you want to.

Scanning is used when you are looking for specific information; an answer to a particular question or a telephone number in a directory.

Skimming is used during step three of the five-step system. You use skimming when you know what you are looking for and want a general impression of what the text contains.

There are different types of skimming depending on what your purpose is:

- **Skimming to overview** – the purpose of this method is to get an outline of what the document is about. You will be looking more at *structure* than at content. This method is used mostly in the second step of the five-step system.

- **Skimming to preview** – this is when you know you are going to re-read the material. Your purpose is to gather as much background information as you can on the subject without spending too much time on it.
- **Skimming to review** – you would use this method when you have already read the material and your purpose is just to re-familiarise yourself with the content.

Successful skimming

Skimming for information is easier when you know where the information is likely to be within the overall scheme of the piece you are reading. While you are speed-reading look for the core information. Once you have stated your purpose for skimming and you know what you are looking for you will be able to identify trigger words that hold the relevant information:

- who
- what
- where
- why
- when
- how

Other key words are those that distinguish fact from opinion. An author might spend the first half of a paragraph giving fact, then you may find words like:

- but
- nonetheless
- however
- yet
- on the other hand

These key words signify that the author is drifting from fact to opinion. If you are looking for an author's opinion on a subject, look for these words.

Practice box

Practice this by going through newspaper or magazine articles with the purpose of identifying the who, what, where, why, when and how as well as the author's opinions, as quickly as you can.

Getting the message

When you read, you convert the information embedded in groups of words into ideas, images, thought, feelings and actions. One of the purposes of reading is getting the message that the words carry. This does not necessarily mean that you have to read all the words. When you speed-read – especially when you start to get used to reading more than one line at a time – you might at first get confused because the words may be presented to you in a different order to the one that was intended. When you read with your eyes, you will find, however, that this does not present a problem because your brain works out what the sentence means regardless of what order the words are in.

Your brain is always trying to make sense of information it receives. When the information you are reading is not complete your brain will naturally fill in the blanks and organise the information so that you can make sense of it. First, read the following sentences *out loud* and work out what they mean:

> We'll twenty minutes in be there.
> Let's dinner for tonight go out.
> Reading visual activity done slowly is only the.

Now, look at the next batch of sentences and get the meaning from them as quickly as you can by looking at the whole sentence and identifying the key words:

> Speed-reading have if you a purpose is easy.
> Have yet holiday you been on this year?
> The improve is to best way to practice.

Which was quicker – reading with your ears or reading with your eyes?

You don't have to have the words in the right order to get the message.

'It's all in the words' – developing a good vocabulary

The bigger your vocabulary, the faster you will be able to read. Hesitating at words you are unfamiliar with wastes time. Unfamiliar terminology makes you think about the whole passage, not just the word. Several questions might go through your head. What does this word mean? Does it change the context? Is it important to my understanding of the text? These questions go through your mind very quickly, but the problem is that once you have answered them you may have forgotten what you have been reading. The real time-waster is when you have to return to the beginning of a passage and start again.

Solving the vocabulary problem is relatively easy, some vocabulary will become clear to you within the context of the paragraph the rest you should look up **before** you begin step five.

> During steps three and four of the five-step system look for unfamiliar words as part of the skimming exercise, then look them up before you begin step five.

Ways of increasing your vocabulary

- Pay attention to new words.
- Keep a small note book where you write down new terminology (with its meaning) that you come across in reading and in conversation.
- Use your new vocabulary.
- Become familiar with the roots of words. If you understand the root, you will be able to work out the meaning of many words. All good dictionaries will show you the roots.

Reading exercises

Here are some exercises to increase your speed-reading rate.

Stretching speed and comprehension
This quick exercise will help improve your memory and increase your speed.

1 Using a pacer, read one page as fast as you can.
2 Stop and write down everything you can remember.
3 Read five pages like this every day, gradually increasing the number of pages you read before you stop to recall what you read.
4 Start with a familiar subject, then, as your ability, confidence and comfort become more apparent to you, take on more challenging material.

Stretching speed
The One-Minute Trip

1 Read for one minute and count how many lines you have read.
2 Continue reading for another minute, reading **two lines more** than you did the first time.
3 In the next minute, read four lines more than you did before, then six, then eight, then ten.
4 Always **read for good comprehension and recall**. As soon as you feel you are not understanding or remembering the text, consolidate at that level until you are comfortable then speed up again gradually.

Reading quickly requires concentration. If you don't understand or remember what you read you may find your concentration drifting because you are becoming disappointed and perhaps bored.

As your concentration improves, stretch the One-Minute Trip to two minutes, then four minutes, then six, and eight … and so on.

Mostly reading
This technique is good for the parts of the text with which

you are already fairly familiar and when you want to be sure you have missed nothing out.

• Read the *first* sentence of the paragraph.
• Skim the rest of the paragraph for key words and, if necessary, read the *last* sentence of the paragraph.

Metronome pacing
You can buy a small electronic metronome at any music shop quite cheaply – it will be a good investment.

Do this exercise for two minutes, then relax for five minutes.

1 Set the metronome at its slowest speed and read one line per 'tick'.
2 Every page or half page increases the pace of the metronome by one, or by as much as you are comfortable with, until you reach the fastest speed on the metronome.
3 Then relax.

The metronome will reach a speed at which you will not be able to read every word. This exercise 'pushes' your eye and brain to see and absorb more than one word at a time, and gradually stretches your ability.

If you drive on a motorway at 70 miles per hour and, as you approach a town, you suddenly have to reduce your speed to 30, you might slow down and think you are travelling at 30 until the police stop you and inform you that you were travelling at 40 or 50 – much faster than you thought.

The similarity between driving and speed-reading doesn't stop there. Travelling at 70 miles an hour you have to concentrate and don't have time to look at the scenery. When speed-reading you are reading so fast that your mind doesn't want to wander as much as it can at '30 miles per hour'.

Summary

What slows you down?

The following are some of the most common speed stoppers with ideas on how to prevent them slowing your reading down.

- **Sub-vocalising (reading with your ears)** is the voice inside your head. The faster you read the less you will sub-vocalise.
- **Vocalising** – If your lips move as you read you are vocalising your text (literally, speaking silently to yourself). This slows you down even more than sub-vocalising: you are limited not only by the pace at which you can speak, but also by how fast you can move your lips.
- **Habit** – Unfortunately most habits are unconscious (you are not aware that you are doing it). They are

easier to rectify once you become aware of them.
To extinguish vocalisation, read with something
safer than a pen between your teeth and you will
soon stop trying to move your lips while you read.
Don't teach children to do this – it could be
dangerous.

What speeds you up?
- Increased concentration by blocking out any noise
  or interference (Tuesday).
- Focus on the task with more than one sense by
  reading actively (Tuesday).
- Push your reading speed faster than you think you
  can read (use a pacer).
- Don't worry about missing out too many words (read
  with your eyes instead of your ears or your mouth).
- Look up words you think you will have difficulty with
  before you start speed-reading (increase your
  vocabulary).

Now that you have improved your base speed-reading rate,
it is time to learn how to remember what you read.

Remember what you read

At the end of a paragraph, chapter or entire book, have you ever had to go back to the beginning because you could not remember what you read? No matter how fast your reading speed is, unless you remember what you read you will have wasted your time.

To remember information for a long time you must *revise*. Revision needs to be *fast*. It would be frustrating if you found yourself spending as much time trying to revise and recall what you read as you did reading it in the first place.

Today, we look at the memory process, how it works and how to get the best from your memory while you read.

- Memory myths
- How memory works – and when it doesn't
- Improving concentration
- Techniques for remembering what you read
- Revision

Memory myths

There is the danger that modern living is overloading the human memory system. There is much more for us to remember than there was for our grandparents. With mass communication growing, more paper being printed than ever before and the emphasis of success moving from physical strength to mental power, we have to develop skills that help us keep up before we can get ahead. The main factor contributing to this overload, however, is not

necessarily the amount of information we are faced with
but rather our *attitude* towards it.

> Stress damages the human memory system more than
> mass information. Access to mass information can be
> stressful – deal with mass information by using
> powerful choosing and reading strategies.

Normally, we are only aware of our memories when we
forget something. It is a big issue for reading because most
people find remembering what they want to remember,
when they read, challenging. This is mainly because they
are not using an appropriate method for retaining the text.

There are some basic myths and assumptions about
memory that need to be considered first.

• Memory is not a stand-alone system. It relies on
  perception, attention and reasoning. Each of these areas
  will be discussed further today.
• Memory is not a system that is based on isolated facts.
  Everything you remember is connected to other pieces of
  information in your memory.
• Memory retrieval relies greatly on association. The more
  organised your memory is, the easier it will be to recall
  information.
• New information is not stored separately from
  old information. Old knowledge helps make sense
  of new information and vice versa that is one reason
  why it is easier to read material you know something
  about.

- Memory is not only designed to store information it is also designed to *use* it.
- We speak about memory as if it is an object. We tend to describe ourselves as having a good, bad or average memory, just like having good or bad lungs. Your memory is not a *thing*. It is certainly not a *single* thing. It's a series of processes that take place throughout your brain, *all the time*.
- Your memory can be trained. It has been said that there are no good or bad memories, just trained or untrained. With very few exceptions, and barring organic damage, everyone is born with a memory that can be developed.

The more you use your memory the stronger it will get. Many of the problems people have with their memories when they grow older are due to lack of mental exercise, lack of physical exercise, poor nutrition, excess stress and/or poor coping strategies.

The basic guideline for improving your memory and ability to concentrate by focusing on physical and mental health is that what is good for the body is also good for the mind.

How memory works – and when it doesn't

There are many models on how the memory system works. Basically, your memory is divided into three parts:

- **Acquisition** – absorbing information
- **Retention** – keeping it in your head
- **Retrieval** – getting it out again

The memory can become unavailable at any point. The trouble is that you only know it is unavailable when you try to retrieve it: you are standing in front of the person whose name you have forgotten trying to introduce him to someone else whose name you have also forgotten.

There are some basic memory rules to follow at each phase to help you remember.

Memory acquisition
The *first rule of acquisition* is **pay attention**. Most of the time we 'forget' something because we didn't have the opportunity to remember it in the first place. Have you ever been told someone's name only to realise two seconds later that you have 'forgotten' it? Chances are your attention was somewhere else. The same phenomenon occurs when you read.

If you have internal talk going on inside you head asking yourself whether you are likely to remember what you are reading or not, the chances are you will not remember much at all.

The *second rule of acquisition* is to **plan**. Before you begin, think of when you are likely to use the information you are reading. Then, decide which memory tool (to be discussed later on today) will help best when the time comes to use the information in the future.

The *third rule of acquisition* is **be interested**. Even if the material seems dull, find something in it that interests you. If you are bored, then parts of your brain will go to sleep and you will find paying attention even more difficult.

The *final rule of acquisition* is **be active**. Read actively. Think about what you read. When you follow the five-step system and you *prepare* to read, take some time in thinking about what you already know on the subject. As we saw from the 'myths and assumptions', your memory does not work in isolation. The more connections you make between the new and old information the easier it will be to understand what you are reading. **Understanding** is the key to **remembering**.

Memory retention
Keeping information in your head is one thing, keeping it there in such a way that you can retrieve it later is a different matter.

Your memory thrives on association and order. The better organised your memory is the easier it will be to retrieve information when you need it. Also, you don't have to keep everything in your head. You can be just as organised on paper as long as you know where to find the information when you need it.

These simple memory tools will help you organise your reading so that retrieval is easy.

Memory retrieval
One reason we have difficulty retrieving information is that we use the wrong method of retrieval. Memories are stored in several parts of your brain. When you try to remember what your front door looks like several areas of your brain will be activated. You might:

- see an internal picture of what your door looks like (visual)
- hear the sound of it closing (auditory)

- recall the last time you walked in or out (kinaesthetic and proprioceptive)
- remember the feeling of the last time you locked yourself out (emotional)
- smell the fresh coat of paint from when you painted it last (olfactory).

When we try to retrieve information we often use only one access point. If you can re-create the whole experience as you remembered it, you will be able to recall more easily.

The importance of concentration
Without concentration there is no memory. Remember the first rule of acquisition – pay attention. Ideas on how to concentrate and avoid the distractions that break up your concentration will be discussed on Thursday. But for now, let's concentrate ...

Concentration does not come easily to many for two reasons:

1 We are very easily distracted.
2 There is much to distract us.

Improving concentration isn't always easy. We don't always have the time or the desire to meditate and practice absolute concentration for several hours each day. Fortunately, there are other ways of getting results.

Improving concentration

Interest and motivation
The more you are interested in what you are doing, the easier it is to concentrate. Remember the last time you were so engrossed in what you were doing that you lost all count of time. Nothing else distracted your attention. You were

totally interested and motivated towards a goal. There are two words to take particular note of – *motivated* and *goal*.

When you know what you are after (a *goal*) and why you are doing it (*motivated*) then the desire (*interest*) to complete the task successfully makes for total concentration.

However, if the job is particularly boring and it is hard to find either motivation or interest, then the *process* is the challenge. Make a decision that, for example:

• Your **goal** is to finish this task as quickly as possible.
• Your **motivation** is that you can get home sooner or get on with another more interesting task.
• Your **interest** is developing a system that will allow you to get through boring material faster and more effectively every time you are faced with it.

Mental numbers
You will be surprised at how easily you can be distracted without realising it is happening. Try this simple experiment: count from one to 26. Notice at what number another thought comes into your head.

Many people will have another thought in their minds by the time they reach five. When you count, it is easy to think of other things and still keep going because counting from one to 26 is a simple exercise. When you are reading, the mental energy needed to focus your attention increases and these drifting thoughts contribute to lack of concentration.

You might like to use the following experiment to increase your concentration.

Simultaneously count from one to 26 and go through the alphabet from A to Z; thus: 1 – A – 2 – B – 3 – C – 4 – D – 5 – E … and so on. Imagine the numbers on the right side of your brain and the letters on the left side. Then switch sides, imagine the numbers on the left side of your brain and the letters on the right.

How fast you can go? How far can you go before you realise your attention has drifted? Once you can go through the alphabet and up to 26 fluently going forwards, try it backwards.

When you feel that your concentration is dipping, do the exercise a few times. It can be quite meditative and relaxing.

Techniques for remembering what you read

There are many ways to remember what you read. Some are listed below. The aim is to be comfortable with all of them and be able to use the right one for the material you are reading. Everyone is different, so experiment with all the approaches.

Linear
Make notes *as* you read or *after* each section. These should include your own thoughts, ideas and cross-references. The more you include your own ideas the stronger your long-term memory will be.

Key words
Highlight the words that carry the message. If you do make notes separately ensure that the key words are correct, so as to avoid having a list of words that make no sense to you when you review the information in the future.

Margin reading

Many people are brought up to believe that books are to be kept in perfect condition. Unless a book is being presented as a priceless antique, it is a form of communication from the author to the reader. You start to take ownership of a book by writing in it or marking it. Underline, circle, highlight essential areas, note your opinions, whether you agree or disagree, and mark what you do or don't understand, and do something about that 'not understanding'. This should *only* be done if the book belongs to you.

Mind-mapping

- Place the key idea in the centre of a horizontal (landscape) page.
- Main ideas form thick branches from the centre.
- Secondary ideas flow from the main ideas.
- Tertiary ideas flow from the secondary ideas.
- And so on until you reach the finest relevant detail.
- Use colours and symbols.
- Use one word or idea per line.

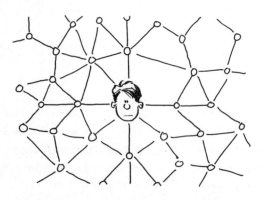

Multi-sensory reading

Do you remember your front door? Do you remember what it sounds like when you close it? What does fresh paint smell like? What does it feel like to be locked out? What colour is it? Multi-sensory reading uses as many of your senses as possible to help you make sense of and absorb the information. Here are some ideas on how to involve your other senses while you read:

- **Sight** – imagine what you are reading in your mind, create a film of the story you are being told.
- **Hearing** – speak to people about the subject; ask questions as you read, teach someone else, make up rhymes and stories.
- **Touch** – draw pictures and symbols representing the information. If the information is something you can do – do it instead of just reading about it.

The more senses you involve in learning new information the easier it will be to recall it because the information will be accessible via more than one function of your brain.

The five-step system and memory support techniques work if you simply use them. The more you practice and the more you become aware of memory, the better you will become.

Revision

A basic guideline is to revise **seven** times in **ten** days.

To remember what you read in the long term, *use*

the information. As mentioned under myths on memory, the memory process is designed for **use** not for storage.

Summary

- Most of what we believe about how our memories work is based on myth.
- Information overload has become a source of stress because we have not learned new coping strategies.
- The four rules of memory acquisition:
  - Pay attention
  - Plan what you have to do
  - Be interested
  - Be active – use all of your senses when you read.
- Understanding is the key to remembering what you are reading.
- Experiment with different ways of remembering what you read. Each text type should be approached differently.

Your eyes and effective reading

The most important tools you have for reading are your eyes.
Any discomfort or strain will affect concentration
immediately. When you are tired or if the lighting is wrong,
you are likely to experience discomfort in your eyes. If your
eyes hurt, a headache may follow quickly. Soon, you may
find you have lost concentration and it is difficult to read. It is
easier to look after your eyes continually, than it is to have to
treat them when something goes wrong owing to bad habits.

Today you will learn:

- How the eyes work when you read
- Reading for comprehension
- The biological challenge
- Reading with your eyes instead of your ears
- How to prevent and cure eyestrain
- Reading from a PC monitor without straining your
  eyes

The exercises in this chapter will give you an idea of what
your eyes do while you read.

How the eyes work when you read

Speed-reading basics
The main reason people read at an average reading rate of
150–250 words per minute is because that is approximately
the rate at which people speak.

While you are reading this paragraph listen to what is

going on inside your head. Do you hear a voice inside your head while you are reading? Are you saying the words inside your mind while you read? This happens because of the way most people are *taught* how to read.

When we are first taught to read we learn to recognise one letter or sound at a time; then, when we have mastered that we move on to recognising one word at a time. The next step is being able to read out loud so that your teacher can see that you have learned to recognise the words accurately. Then you are left to read 'to yourself'.

That is how the inner voice most of us have in our heads while we read becomes a habit. Instead of reading out loud we read silently. So when we talk about reading with your *ears* instead of your eyes – that is how it happens. You learn that you have to *hear* the words rather than *see* them to understand what you are reading.

When you read 'to yourself', you read in your head at the **same rate** as when you were reading out loud. At the beginning, reading 'to yourself' is quite slow because you are still learning to recognise the words fluently and as you read more and go further into the education system your reading rate increases because your vocabulary increases. But your reading **strategy** doesn't change.

As long as you are reading by saying each word to yourself in your mind, you will only ever be able to read as fast as you can speak – which for most people is between 150 and 250 words per minute.

You can only hear or say one thing at a time but you can **see** millions of things at a time. Learning to speed-read is about learning to read with your eyes instead of your ears.

Reading is the slowest visual exercise we do. Look outside the nearest window for three seconds then close your eyes and say what you saw. How long did it take you to **see** what you saw and how long did it take you to **say** what you saw? Speaking to yourself when you read is the same as looking at a spectacular view or watching a film and instead of visually understanding it, translating what you see into words that take several times longer to form, communicate and understand.

Visual and auditory memory is in different parts of the brain. When you first start to learn how to read with your eyes instead of your ears, your comprehension will diminish. This is perfectly normal. After a few hours of practice (in the beginning) and maybe 15 minutes a day for a few days you will find comprehension returning to what it was and more long-term and integrated than you ever had it before. The same happens, for example, when you learn to touch type instead of looking at the keyboard and typing with one finger.

Reading for comprehension

The aim of speed-reading is to learn how to 'read' more than one word at a time. To do that, you have to read with your eyes instead of your ears. As well as increasing the speed at which you read, your comprehension increases. When you read more than one word at a time you read *phrases* rather than isolated words. **The meaning the author wants to put across is in the phrase not the isolated word**. Meaning is in *groups* of words so the more you are able to comprehend at one time the better your comprehension, understanding and subsequent recall will be. You understand more because you are reading in terms of ideas, thoughts and images rather than isolated words that mean nothing in themselves.

An exercise later today will help you increase your confidence in reading with your eyes instead of your ears.

The biological challenge

Your eyes move very fast. They can process large amounts of information rapidly. If you read slowly, your eyes will tend to wander. The pacer will go a long way to help preventing that. Remember the exercise you did on Monday that showed you how differently your eyes moved when they had something to follow? Go back and refresh your memory if you need to.

Some eye movements you can do something about, some you can't.

Fixation time
Your eyes need a certain amount of time to be able to absorb information. Try this experiment next time you are a passenger in a car. As you drive, keep your eyes fixed on one point, not letting them settle on anything flying by the window. Does your view become blurred? Next, as you go, pick out certain parts of the landscape and follow them briefly. You might notice that what you look at becomes clear while the background is blurred. The same applies to reading. Your eyes need to rest – albeit it briefly – on groups of words, to be able to see them. The more words you can see and recognise in a single visual 'byte' the faster you will be able to read.

Peripheral vision
Try an experiment: place your finger on the middle of the page and see as much as you can – where you are sitting, the room you are in, your surroundings. Your peripheral vision gives you the ability to see an enormous amount in a single visual byte. Now, without moving your eye from middle of the page, try to read the words on the edges of the page.

How did you do?

You will find that although you can see the words, you might not be able to 'read them'. When you were taught how to read you were taught to focus on one word at a time and not a whole line. Being able to expand what you can recognise within your peripheral vision takes practice. There are some exercises later in this section that will help you increase peripheral perception – you can do some of them while walking down the street.

Regression and progression
These are visual tics. They are the result of poor concentration and lack of confidence in your memory. *Regression* refers to the habit of going back to previous words or paragraphs to make sure you have understood them or remembered them accurately. *Progression* refers to the habit of jumping forwards for no particular reason.

Studies were done in the USA on how people's eyes moved when they read. Groups of people were given texts to read. At the bottom of the test piece was the figure $3,000,000.00. Every single person's eyes moved to the bottom of the text before they had read half the page to see what the $3,000,000.00 figure was all about. In terms of wasting time several things happen when you do this.

- You forget what you have just read.
- Your comprehension drops because you are reading something out of context.

Reading with a pacer and following the five-step system will help to reduce these reading habits. The following exercises will help you further.

Increasing your span of recognition within your peripheral vision
Exercise directions:
In the pyramid of numbers and letters on the following pages, focus on the hash mark down the centre of the pyramid. The aim is to see how much you can read in your peripheral perception. Write down what you can see. Note: don't move your eyes from the centre row. You will be tempted to focus on the end of the row, but for the purpose of the exercise try to keep your eye on the centre hash. You might notice several things.

- You might not be able to see some of the letters and numbers on the longer lines. This is quite normal. Your optic nerve enters your eye at that point creating a 'blind spot'.
- If your eyes are of equal strength, you may find that you can see more to the right of centre than you can to the left. This is because we read from left to right and our eyes are conditioned to look in that direction for new text. If you were brought up reading Arabic or Hebrew, you might find that you will be able to see more to the left instead of the right of centre.

Exercise 1:
Place your pacer on the hash and move it down the hash marks in the centre of the pyramid. Keep your eye in the centre. Write down what you see on either side of the hash mark without moving your eyes away from the centre.

S # p
2 E # 7 e
d R 8 # E 5 a
D 2 5 I 5 # n G 5 8 9
6 B 2 9 o 6 3 # R 8 3 4 2 N 1
3 9 g 9 2 E 5 4 n # 8 5 2 i 4 u S 7

Exercise 2:
Follow the instructions in exercise one. Keep your eye on the central column of letters and write down what you can see on either side.

WG	H	PF
KD	T	OL
VS	K	DA
YO	E	NL
PZ	R	NJ
5S	I	B9

Exercise 3:
Repeat the above instructions, with the following columns.

only if	armbands	existed but
once a	bee	swam in
a three	legged	race he
got half	way	to the other
end of the	beer glass	but was

Did you find the words any easier to read than the random letters? The words didn't make much sense either. Try this next exercise.

Exercise 4:

Beginning to read more than one word at a time: read the text as quickly as possible, keeping your eyes in the middle of the pyramid.

A
beetle
loved a
certain hare
And wandered with him
everywhere:
They went to fairs
and feasts together,
Took walks in any kind of weather,
Talked of the future
and the past
On sunny days or overcast,
But since their friendship was so pleasant,
Lived for the most part in the present.
From 'The Eagle and the Beetle', by Vikram Seth

Reading with your eyes instead of your ears

This next exercise will illustrate to you the difference between reading with your ears or your eyes. The more you practice it the better you will get at trusting what you see without having to hear it.

Exercise 5:

Recognition exercise.

1 Cut a piece of fairly thick card about 2 cm square.
2 Place the card over the letters and flash the letter as quickly as you can.

3 Cover the letters and 'flash' them as fast as you can, then write what you see in the adjacent column.
4 Try to keep the pace at which you reveal the numbers and letters to yourself constant.

143	Emc2	tdp		inki	
I46	Lsp5	3Pq	......	blt9	......
Heg	wini	olp		wom8	
37R	rQwg	3owm	......	286r	......
63I	6The	tap		unIw	
53L	Hare	cim	......	te4q	......
Jo4	M23p	536		wim2	
ThR	Luck	592	......	241y	......
2h7	7play	per		tolp	
Jon	u89Un	ith	......	154r	......
8Em	Pking	kin		tosi	
Em2	43Jub	min	......	90Pp	......
492	krimb	map		76yz	
hEp	HatrP	43T	......	jipx	......

- Which column was easiest to do?
- Did you find that sometimes you mistook an 'S' for a '5'?
- Did you find the double lines more challenging than the single lines?
- Most important – did you find that the letters that most resembled words were immediately recognisable and easy to recall?

When you read with your eyes you don't need to hear the whole word in your mind to know what it says. Your brain only needs a portion of the word to be able to make sense of it.

Develop your own eye exercises and practice them as often as you have time to. If you are going to choose one exercise to develop your visual reading for your 21-day programme (see Saturday) then exercise five should be it.

Peripheral vision and awareness

As you walk, look straight ahead and try to 'see' as much as you can in your whole visual range. Try to see what is to the extreme left or right, top or bottom of your visual field. As you go, articulate what you see. After you have done this for a while sit down and read, using your guide, as fast as you can and see the difference in the speed and ease of your reading. This is an excellent exercise to do while you are walking through town or a park.

How to prevent and cure eyestrain

Your eyes need rest. The more relaxed they are the longer you will be able to read for. Here are a few simple things you should do to prevent and cure eyestrain.

- Even before you feel tired, rest your eyes by **closing them** for a few moments every ten or fifteen minutes.
- As often as you remember to, **palm**. Palming is an excellent eye-relaxing exercise. Rub your hand together until they are warm, then close your eyes and cover them with your hands so that no light gets in. Do not press against your eyeballs: if you were to do so you could damage them. Cover your eyes like this for as long as you have time to.
- **Blink** – The scratchy feeling in your eyes is probably there because they are dry. Many people who have eye problems compound them by not blinking and watering the eyes. While you are reading (especially from a PC monitor) be aware of your eyes and blink often. If it helps, put a sign above your PC reminding yourself to blink.
- If your eyes feel particularly tired, there are a number of very good **eye washes** you can get from any pharmacy. Follow the instructions carefully when you use them. Check with your optician or your doctor.
- If you wear **contact lenses** it is even more important to take care of your eyes while you are reading. If you have a lot of reading to do it might be advisable to take them out. Carry a pair of glasses with you so that you can swap.
- When you read, your eyes are limited to how much they move. An excellent way to relieve stress is to practice some **eye-robics**. First, look straight ahead, then look up as far as you can, down as far as you can, to the left and to the

right. Then, look to the top left, top right, bottom
right and bottom left. Hold each gaze for only a
second or so. When you have done that, squeeze
your eyes shut and if you want to, repeat the
exercise. After you have completed the exercise,
palm for a few minutes.

NEVER rub your eyes directly on the eyeball. There is
nothing to protect the eye from damage when you do that.

Reading from a PC monitor without straining your eyes

There is much you can do to make reading from a monitor
less stressful on your eyes. Here are a few tips.

- **Font size and type** – If someone has sent you a
  document and the font is difficult to read either due to its
  size or type, change it.
- **Screen contrast** – Make sure the background contrasts
  the text on the screen. Sometimes a white screen might
  be too strong and a blue one too dark. A pale blue screen
  is quite a good one to read from.
- **Screen interference** – Have as little around your screen
  as possible. Sometimes it is tempting to have all the icons
  on display. The more you have around your screen, the
  smaller the screen space is. Only have what is necessary
  for the work you are doing.
- **Screen savers** – There are screen savers on the market
  now that remain active all the time. The one that held my
  attention for quite some time was a sheep that ran
  around my screen while I worked. Not only does it help to

relax your eyes and prevents you from staring at the screen, but a sheep chasing frogs across the screen is good for your sense of humour and anything good for your sense of humour is good for your stress levels which in turn is good for concentration.

- **Screen position** – Keep the screen a comfortable distance away from you. It should be at least arm's length away. Also, avoid having the screen right in front of a window. The contrast in light can be uncomfortable and the activity outside can be distracting.
- **Comfort** – working at a PC means that the only part of your body that gets any exercise are your fingers. Stop, stretch your body and do the eye-robics every 20 to 30 minutes.

Summary

- A pacer helps you read more with your eyes than with your ears.
- As long as you read with your ears, you will only be able to read as fast as you can speak.
- Reading more than one word at a time allows you to understand chunks of meaning rather than individual words.
- Regression and progression are visual tics that are a result of poor concentration and a lack of confidence in your memory. A pacer will eliminate these habits.
- Look after your eyes continually. As soon as they feel uncomfortable, stop and take a break.
- Take special care of your eyes if you work from a VDU for extended periods of time.

Distractions and solutions

In an ideal world we would read only what interests us, in a perfect environment, with as much time as we needed, when we wanted to. However, life is not like that. We sometimes have to read material we are not particularly interested in, at a time and place not suited to our reading style, and all too often with a deadline.

Distractions are not just what happens around you. Your internal state can be just as distracting as a constantly ringing telephone. Distractions hamper effective reading and accurate recall. The more you can reduce them the more chance you will have of successfully reading what you need to in the time available.

Today, we will look at a range of distractions and at ways of working around them.

The distractions you will solve are:

- Lack of concentration
- External distractions
- Internal distractions
- Physical distractions
- Environmental issues
- Work distractions
- People demanding your attention
- Clearing your desk of distractions
- Vocabulary

Lack of concentration

If your attention drifts easily, inconsequential things
distract you and you find it hard to concentrate, an easy
solution may exist.

We discussed concentration and focus on Tuesday. If you
think it might be helpful to go back to refresh your
memory, try one of Tuesday's concentration exercises. The
following tips will help increase your concentration and
your ability to focus on one task.

- To ensure peak concentration, **take breaks often** –
  approximately five minutes every 30 minutes if you are
  only reading. If you are reading a number of different
  texts and taking notes you could stretch your reading time
  to between 45 minutes and one hour before you take a
  five or ten minute break. Pay attention to your body as
  you read. When you start yawning, making mistakes, re-
  reading passages or developing a headache it is time for
  a break. If you work through the symptoms of tiredness,

your concentration, ability to remember and to understand what you are reading will diminish rapidly. Taking a break does not mean lying down and going to sleep for twenty minutes (although that does help) – go for a walk, drink some water, do something different.

- Know your **reasons for reading**. On Sunday and Monday, we discussed the importance of knowing why you are reading something. The clearer your purpose, the easier it will be to concentrate. As with many things in life – if you know what your reasons are for doing something, it is easier to do it, even when you do not really want to. If you have no reason, however, you are likely to give up fairly quickly.

- **Read actively** using a pacer, especially if you are feeling tired or if the material is challenging. The more senses you use, the more alert you are likely to remain. Imagine eating a meal and all you could do was see it. You couldn't smell it, taste it, feel the texture of the food or hear the sounds of cutting and slicing a juicy dish. All you could do was see it and eat it. How much do you think you would enjoy that meal? 80% of the enjoyment is in the sensory appreciation of the meal: the taste, smell, texture and presentation of the food. The same applies to reading. Unfortunately, we are taught at a very early age to appreciate reading only through *one* sense. When you start building mind-maps, taking notes, thinking, discussing and actively reading, you will find that reading becomes more like the meal you can see, taste, smell, hear and feel. You almost always remember a good meal when the company is good and the surroundings pleasant. Treat reading like a good meal – you'll be surprised.

- Set a definite **time limit**. Break your reading into chunks. The chunks should be small enough to feel easily managed and big enough to feel that you are achieving your goal. Be realistic. If, as you read, you find that the size of the chunks is too big or too small, stop and re-assess. Be flexible.

External distractions

Some people can concentrate either because of, or in spite of, background noise. If you are not one of them, do everything you can to minimise the noise around you. Unfortunately, there is some external noise that you don't have much control over. If you work in an open-plan office you might find the noise in the office distracting. There are several things you can do to minimise distraction from this kind of noise.

- **Earplugs** – if you get the right type they can be very comfortable and effective. Most good chemists will supply them. Try out a few makes and then keep a few sets on your desk.
- Wear earphones with **appropriate music**. Music without words and not too loud. Baroque music is best for maximum concentration; approximately 55–60 beats per minute. Make sure it's not too melancholy and only play music you enjoy. Mozart, Vivaldi and some of Beethoven's works are also good for concentration. Experiment with music. Put one composer on for 20 minutes, change to another and then compare how you feel or how well you concentrated.
- If your desk is in a truly **open-plan space** – no dividers

between the desks – creating a visual barrier between you and the rest of the space will help cut distraction. You do not have to build a wall around you, this is not always desirable or possible. All you need do is place something on your desk that reaches eye level. This will provide a psychological barrier between you and the distracting environment and make it easier to cope with.

- If at all possible, leave the noisy environment and find a **quiet space** to read in. A delegate in one of my workshops would go into the cleaning closet when he had a very important document to read that needed all of his attention. He would go into the closet, jam the door shut, read the document, take the notes he needed and when he was finished he would come out. It worked for him and he was lucky enough to have a cleaning closet nearby with plenty of light and a bit of space, a supply of fresh air and no fumes.

Internal distractions

Internal noise is caused by your mind wandering, perhaps because you have not decided to spend the time on a particular task. The guidelines on concentration will help you here. But what will help most is the *decision* to take the time and read.

If you don't make a firm decision to sit down and read, the type of internal talk that goes through your head might sound like this: 'I don't have the time for this ... X really needs to be done now ... Y will have to move to this afternoon ... I should be doing Z ...' There will be so much 'noise' in your head that you will be unlikely to remember one word you have read and will be wasting time.

- Make a decision to allocate a certain amount of time to read a set amount of material. If you can plan it into your day, do so. Some reading cannot be planned for. In this instance, instead of diving into the text without thinking, take time, go through the preparation and preview stages quickly. Then, if you feel that the document does need to be read, decide when you are going to do it and when you will put the time aside.
- When the decision is made, most other internal talk will disappear and you will be able to focus.

Physical distractions

Tired
When you are tired you will find it almost impossible to concentrate. If you can take a break and go for a short nap or walk in the park, do so. If you are unable, there are several other strategies open to you.

- Cut the time you spend reading down to ten- to 15-minute chunks.
- Use multi-sensory reading.
- Drink plenty of water
- Do aerobic exercises during your breaks – jump up and down a bit to get the oxygen flowing.
- Breathe deeply and stretch every few minutes.
- If you have music playing make it upbeat and energetic.
- Make sure you have a *very good reason* for reading through your tiredness.
- Do not go on more than you have to – stop when you are finished and take a good rest.
- Avoid working through the night.
- Avoid sugar or starch.
- Avoid caffeine. For optimum performance you want to be alert not jittery.
- Reading at the right time of day can go a long way to preventing tiredness. You may notice that you can concentrate better at certain times of the day. Your results will be better if you read at those times.

Sore eyes

Any kind of physical discomfort is a distraction. Your eyes are your primary tool for reading, so take care of them. For more details on eye care while reading, refresh your memory on Wednesday's summary.

Stress and reading

If you are stressed it is better to stop for a moment even if you feel you don't have the time. Stop, breathe, relax,

evaluate the job, have a cup of tea or water and carry on.
Being stressed does not make you read any faster or more
effectively.

Hunger and thirst

Hunger is a serious distraction. Similarly, if you eat too
much, your concentration will be equally badly affected.
If you have a large amount of reading to do, avoid
eating too much at once and avoid excess sugar and
starch. Another cause of poor concentration is
dehydration. Your body is 90% water and needs to be
constantly replenished. When you feel thirsty, you are
already dehydrated, so drink a lot of water even if you
don't feel you need to.

Environmental issues

Comfort

Ensure that you have fresh air and adequate light. Make
yourself as comfortable as possible without feeling
sleepy.

Light

Daylight is best. If there is none, then there should not be too much contrast between the levels of light under which you are working and the rest of the room. This helps prevent eye strain. The main source of light should come over the shoulder opposite to your writing hand.

Desk and chair

Make sure your desk and chair are the right height. When you are on your chair you should be able to sit back, with the chair supporting your back with your feet flat on the floor. If you cannot reach the floor place a block at your feet. Your desk should be large enough to take everything you need for the work you are undertaking.

Work distractions

- **Plan your day**. Distractions come easily when you don't know what you want to achieve. At the start of your day write down everything you want to achieve including the reading you want to do. Set aside time for it. It might also be useful to put time aside in your plan for leisure reading. Once you plan it in and can see that reading a novel for a while isn't going to mean that you will not achieve everything else in your day, you will find that you enjoy the time, still get everything done and improve your speed-reading by reading more.
- **Set ground rules**. Once you start something, don't let anything distract you from completing it unless there is a very good reason. Have you ever started

mowing the lawn or doing the dishes only to get distracted onto something else and then find you don't really want to go back to it? Once you start something, *finish it*. This will not only improve the quality of your work, it will also increase the quantity of what you can achieve. You will also feel more relaxed and at ease because the job has been done.

People demanding your attention

Few people have the luxury of being able to work without interruptions. There will always be someone, somewhere demanding your attention at some point, whether by phone, in person or by email.

If you can, set aside the time you need to read and put up a 'do not disturb' notice.

If you are unable to do that, and most of us are, deal with interruptions like phone calls and people wanting to see you by consciously breaking off from your reading task and paying attention to the interruption.

If the phone rings or someone comes up to you while you are reading:

- finish the sentence or paragraph you are on, if at all possible
- place a mark on the place where you stopped
- briefly revise in your mind or on paper your understanding of the last sentence you read
- then, give attention to the next task.

Once the interruption is over, you can return to your reading, by:

- sitting for a moment to recall your understanding of the last sentence you read
- re-affirming your intention and purpose for reading
- setting the time again for a manageable chunk
- then, continuing to read.

Habit dictates that when we are interrupted we are very likely to 'hop' from one task to another. Taking a brief pause between tasks will ensure that you don't waste time trying to find where you left off. When you go back to your reading you will be able to begin immediately instead of having to sort out your ideas and remove confusion from your mind.

Clearing your desk of distractions

- **Mail** – If you get a lot of mail at the beginning of the day have a routine of 20 minutes maximum each day to open all your mail and file it, deal with it or bin it. Don't let anything get in the way of doing that. It might not seem an important job at the time but when a week's mail piles up on your desk undealt with it, can be very distracting and waste more time than a short stress-free period set aside every day.

- **Desk space** – Every piece of paper on your desk will distract you several times every day. To minimise this type of distraction make sure that the only things on your desk are those that have something to do with the project in hand. If you have your 'in' and 'out' trays on your desk, find another place for them for a week. At the end of the week, assess how differently you spend your time. When the tray is on your desk, all you have to do is look up and you will see everything else you have to do that day, instead of being able to focus on one job at a time.

- **Clutter** – If your desk tends to be full of paper, clear it of *everything* other than the job at hand – for just one day – and see the difference. At the end of each day, make sure you leave your desk totally clear. In the morning you will feel far more relaxed and able to choose what you want to deal with instead of having to deal with whatever happens to be on the top of the pile.

- **Other people's reading** – Do not let anyone put anything on your desk that you haven't seen or agreed to have there, especially if you have to read it. When someone gives you something to read ask them to clearly explain why they think you have to read it and then decide if you want to accept it as an activity in your schedule. If they cannot give you an answer, think carefully before you accept it because once you have, you will be committed to doing it.

Vocabulary

The better your vocabulary the faster you will be able to read. For more details see Monday's section on speed-reading.

Summary

To ensure peak concentration:

- Take breaks often.
- Make sure you have a reason for reading.
- Read actively.
- Set a definite time limit for your reading.
- Wear earplugs or earphones if the noise around you is distracting.
- If possible, find a quiet space to read, if you have something that requires your full attention.
- Be aware of what you eat and drink while you work. Your diet has a great affect on your ability to concentrate.
- Take care of your eyes.
- Plan your day and leave space for unexpected demands on your time.
- Work in a clear space. Have only the paperwork relating to the job at hand on your desk.
- Avoid accepting reading material from people until you are sure you have to read it.
- Spend a maximum of 20 minutes a day sorting through your mail and email.

Reading different types of material for different reasons

We have looked at the five-step reading system, speed-reading, memory development, how your eyes work and how to avoid distractions. Now it's time to look at what you read and how to apply different reading techniques, to ensure you get the most out of the reading.

Today, we will cover:

- Reading different types of material
- Making the most of your available time
- How to get the message in the minutes before a meeting
- Finding the right information fast
- The real world – reading under pressure

Reading different types of material

The way you approach a document (book, newspaper, memo, etc) should be driven by your purpose.

Technical material
This type of reading can be fairly easy because most technical writing will be well structured. Also, it will be rare that you have to read and remember everything about the text without being able to refer to it later on when you need it. For this type of reading apply the five-step system in its entirety and use a memory system that works well for you. Use mind-maps. If you don't like mind-maps, try a process map. This technique allows you to see how information,

ideas and practices are linked and what effect they have on each other.

Non-fiction for leisure
This is probably the easiest of all reading simply because you are interested in the subject. Most non-fiction, like technical writing, is also fairly well structured so the five-step process can be readily applied.

It is easy to become absorbed in 'work'-related reading and not put time aside for leisure reading and knowledge gathering. Once you are comfortable with speed-reading and the five-step process, you will find that non-fiction is the ideal material to practice on. Enjoy taking the time for this type of reading. If you have 'work' to do, you might feel uncomfortable or guilty about taking time out for leisure albeit non-fiction reading. A good way to get around this is to make part of your purpose increasing your reading skill so that you will be able to read 'work' material more effectively. Besides, if you only ever read text that bores you, your passion for reading will soon be subdued. Make the time to read what you want to read.

Reading for study
More and more people are studying as well as coping with a full-time job. Here is a way to structure your reading so that you succeed without causing yourself undue stress and giving up your life for a few years.

- Determine how many study days you have before the exam or end of the course. Be realistic about this. If you are working full time as well as studying, then remember that you will only have mornings, evenings and weekends and that you also have to fit a life in somewhere.

- Establish exactly what you have to study. Generally you will have a number of books, perhaps a few cassette tapes, a few television programmes, and some notes from lectures. Gather all the material together into one place so that you can see that the amount of information you have to learn is finite. This does the soul good.
- Go through the course notes and make a list of all the different areas you have to cover.
- Under each heading write down the chapters, tapes, videos and lectures (all sources) you have to refer to for information.
- Organise the headings in an 'information order'. Some areas of a subject serve as good background for others so cover those first. The order you study the areas in is entirely up to you and dependent on your current knowledge base.
- Once all areas are covered, the sources are identified, and the areas put into sequence, you should create a realistic and achievable timetable.
- The timetable you create should not have you starting at 4 am and beginning again as soon as you get home. You will burn out. Make space in your timetable for Quality Recover Time (QRT). Have plenty of it.
- Create a good study space. This space should only be used for study if possible.
- Enjoy the learning process by rewarding yourself for each accomplishment (at least once a day).

Reading for research
The good thing about reading for research is that your purpose is very clearly defined and you are looking for something quite specific. Apply the five-step system and follow the guidelines for 'reading for study'.

Reading for work (especially mail and memos)
The rule here is 'be selective'. The trouble with reading that you do for work is that there will probably be a resulting activity for each document. Before you read anything, especially if it is likely to take you a while or if it seems to land on your desk often, ask a few questions first:

- Who wants you to read it?
- Why do they want you to read it?
- What do you have to do with the information once you have read it?

Once you have ascertained that there are good reasons for you reading the documents, take the following steps:

- Decide how much time you are going to spend reading incoming mail or memos.
- Preview the documents with one thing in mind – can this go in the bin? Then sort them into two piles – one of which goes straight into the bin, the other which requires further attention.
- Passive read or skim all of the documents in the remaining pile and ask one question of each – can this be filed or does it require action? Put the pile for filing aside to file.
- Actively read the remaining pile and, using post-it notes or writing directly on the letter or document, write what actions need to be taken.

- Finally, plan the actions into your day or week and file the documents into the appropriate file so that you can retrieve them easily when you need them.

Remember the clear desk policy – only have papers on your desk for the job you are currently working on.

Newspapers
NOTE – this does not apply to the casual relaxed Sunday morning reading of the paper unless you want it to. Reading a newspaper should be approached with as much consideration as reading anything else. The five-step system works very well for papers. It is not necessary to go through the entire five-step process in order. You can read a paper very quickly by following three very simple steps.

1 *State your purpose* – are you reading to get an overview of the whole paper or are you looking for a particular story?
2 *Preview and passive read* (read headlines and first paragraphs) the entire paper, circling the articles you would like to return to.
3 *Actively read* selected articles for the information you want.

REMEMBER – these are only suggested guidelines. If you find another way of reading a paper even faster, then use whatever works for you.

Magazines
Reading a magazine (especially special interest or trade magazines) is slightly different to reading a newspaper. A newspaper is one of many sources of news. If you miss

anything from the paper, you could get the story from the television, radio or Internet. Most magazines only come out once a month or once a quarter. A magazine should thus be treated like a small textbook. Follow all the steps of the five-step reading system to get the best out of a magazine. If there is information you are likely to need again in the magazine there are several things you can do to make it easily accessible.

- Read the magazine with post-it notes to hand. As you find articles you are interested in, note the page number, title and brief summary (just a sentence or two) on the post-it note. Stick the post-it on the front page of the magazine and file it in a file dedicated to 'interesting articles'.
- If you don't want to keep the whole magazine then tear out the pages or photocopy the articles you want and file those away with a brief summary of what the article is about and what you might use it for later.

Emails

Emails are a blessing or a curse depending on who is sending them. Rule one with emails is to do to others, as you want them to do to you. If you don't want huge letters and memos and masses of junk mail – don't send it! If you have someone who keeps sending you emails you don't want, whether it's jokes or stories, be firm and ask them not to. Like traditional mail, if you can see it is junk before you open the envelope – bin it.

A good way of viewing email is to have the feature on your system where your inbox screen is split. The top half has a list of all the messages, and the bottom half lets you read the email without actually opening it. This saves time.

If there are attachments to the email and you need to read them fast then it might be better to print them out. If you prefer to read from the screen there are some ideas on Wednesday on how to do that without straining your eyes.

Novels
The more you read the faster you will become. Reading novels is excellent practice for speed-reading skills. Your reading rate will automatically increase when you are aware of your reading strategy and practice the reading system on non-fiction.

Making the most of your available time

The most important thing about reading (for work or study, this does not apply to leisure reading unless you want it to) is planning. These are simple guidelines on how to make the most of your time.

- Read when you are feeling alert and refreshed. If you have to read and you are tired, drink plenty of water and take regular breaks.
- Plan what you have to read and set aside a little more time than you think you will need.
- When someone puts something on your desk expecting you to read it find out whether it is really necessary and whether someone can summarise it for you rather than reading the whole document yourself.
- Make the bin the first option when you are sorting mail (including email).
- When you are going through your mail decide what you have to read and put non-urgent documents aside. If you have time at the end of the day to read them, then do so.

How to get the message in the minutes before a meeting

'I only have five minutes and I have to sound like I know what I'm talking about.' Have you ever been in the situation where someone gives you a document and tells you that you are expected at a meeting in five minutes to discuss it with others who have probably had a day to read it?

Do you find that your mind goes blank and for some reason words and letters don't make sense anymore? This has more to do with stress and a lack of strategy than it does with time. When this happens:

1 Ask them what it has to do with you – ask for background information.

2 Ask them why you only have five minutes – this gives purpose and focus.
3 Ask them to briefly summarise the text for you – this gives you content.

Once you have done that complete steps one to four of the five-step system:

1 State your purpose – why do you have to read this? What are you going to do with the information?
2 Flick through the text reading any summaries and conclusions.
3 Read through it again, this time looking for key words, significant figures or words in bold or italics.
4 Read the first and last paragraphs of each section.
5 If there is time fill in the gaps by reading as much as you can beginning with the first sentence of each paragraph and any bullet points (see step four of the five-step system).

VERY IMPORTANT

As you go through steps one to four take notes, preferably on the document itself. The thoughts you have as you read will probably be what you would want to contribute to the meeting. If you don't write them down you might forget and lose valuable insights.

Going into the meeting
Before you go into the meeting, stop at the door, stand up straight, breathe in deeply and smile (relax). Once inside:

- Don't profess to be the expert on the subject.
- Listen first to what others have to say.

- Ask questions before you make statements.

You could bluff if others know less than you do but eventually you will be caught out. It's easier to find a reading strategy that gives you a chance of absorbing as

much information as possible rather than struggling to look as if you know what you are talking about.

Once you take control you will relax and be able to concentrate on the task successfully.

Finding the right information fast

When you have to find information fast, use steps one, two and three of the five-step system.

1   Be very clear about what you are looking for.
2   Write your purpose down.
3   Begin step two (preview) by highlighting any chapters or sections that look like they could contain the answers to your question. Use post-it notes to mark the relevant pages with a comment on them as to what you expect to find there.

4 Once completed, begin step three by re-stating and re-
   clarifying your purpose. What exactly are you looking
   for and what are the key words that would alert you to
   the answer?
5 Passively read (skim or scan) the pieces of text you
   identified during the preview stage.
6 Stop as soon as you find your answer unless you *decide*
   to continue.

When you read a document for the first time, read it with
the intention of going back to it to find information at a
later date. Mark relevant pages or take referencing notes.
Writing a brief summary of each section in the margins is
an excellent way to help you access information later. It is
also a very good technique for remembering what you have
read.

The real world – reading under pressure

Sometimes there is not enough time to read what you have
to. When this happens (and for some people it could be
happening every day) you have to be disciplined about
what you read and develop excellent prioritisation skills.

A deadline can be one of the biggest distractions. Becoming
wound up and stressed only defeats the object. When you
have such a situation:

1 Make a realistic assessment of the available time.
2 Decide what you **have to know**.
3 Decide where the best and fastest source of information is.
4 If it is something you have to read, complete steps one to
   three of the five-step system and be very clear about
   cutting out what is not essential.

5 Speak to someone who already knows something on the subject and gather as much information as possible.
6 Find out exactly why you have such a tight deadline and find out whether it can be changed.
7 After your questions have been answered, divide your reading into the amount of time you have, and focus, relax, breathe deeply, make sure you have a good supply of water.
8 Take plenty of breaks. When you are under pressure it is more important to sit back and take stock than when you have all the time in the world. If you are under pressure and not taking care of yourself, stress will counteract all the work you are doing.

To avoid this happening repeatedly, it is important to be able to prioritise your reading and other tasks.

Summary

- The reading and memory strategies you use will vary depending on what you are reading and why you are reading it. Treat every text differently.
- Take time to plan your reading even if you only have a few minutes to go over something briefly.
- Prioritise your reading.

What next?

Finally, today, we will be learning and developing new methods and turning them into habits.

- Guidelines for a 21-day programme
- 21-day table
- Summary of the five-step system
- A to Z of effective reading

Guidelines for a 21-day programme

Whenever you learn something new there is a period of time when you know that you know how to do it but you haven't quite got it right yet. This is a most fragile time in learning. Receiving the information is easy – you read a book, go to a course, listen to a tape. Once the information is in your head, it's up to you. Do you use the information or do you not? Do you put your course books on the shelf until 'later' or not? Do you put the book back on the bookshelf and think – 'hmmm, interesting' – and get back to your old habits? What you *do* with your new information is entirely up to you. You can either forget about it or fully integrate what you have learnt into the way you live, work and study.

It takes decision and action. The decision takes a split second. Are you going to become the best you can be?

After you make such a decision it is important to build a plan. Sometimes, when we are about to start something new we believe that it is the only way to go and everything else in our lives must change to suit the new way. The problem is that when you try to change old habits, they fight back. One way of making the change process easy is to create a daily plan. Instead of doing everything in one day and being overwhelmed, complete the task a bit at a time.

The first time I created one of these programmes I put aside four hours a day to the new task. The day started at 5 am and at 9 am I would have breakfast, go for an energised run and get on with the day. I lasted two days. I started too early, spent too long at it, crammed too much into the time and spent the rest of the day half asleep and a bit irritable.

Rules for the 21-day programme are generally common sensical.

- **Make your programme not too easy, not too difficult**. The programme you create must be easy enough for you to know it is achievable and challenging enough to excite you.
- **Select topics that interest you**. The material you read to develop your speed-reading skills should be interesting to you. During your normal working day you may come across plenty that you have to read that isn't too interesting.
- **Have variety**. On one day, practice speed-reading with a novel, the next day, try a newspaper, after that practice with magazines you have wanted to read for a while. Each time the aim is to read as much as possible, using the most effective technique possible.
- **Put aside 20 minutes each day to practice speed-reading exercises (see Monday)**. 20 minutes is a guideline. If you only have ten minutes then that would do fine as long as every day you are spending some focused time working on your new skill. The best time to do this is in the morning because it will remind you to pay attention to your reading as the day goes by. If you can only put 20 minutes aside in the evening then remind yourself in the morning when you plan your day that you have put that time aside and that you will be aware of your reading throughout the day.
- **Integrate your new knowledge into what you already do during the day**. Use your new skill every time you read something: your mail, letters, newspapers, books, emails, memos, the backs of cereal boxes – anything.

- **Keep your purpose clear**. If you do not have a purpose you will quickly lose interest. Keep in mind *why* you are learning how to read fast. What else do you want to do with the extra time you have? What will speed-reading give you? Why did you pick up *Successful Speed-reading in a week* in the first place?
- **Practice daily**. The more consistent your practice is the better you will become. If you speed-read on one day and forget for the next few the chances are that the days between practicing will just increase.
- **Teach someone else**. When you can teach someone else what you have learnt, you have learnt it well. If you have children, teach them – any time is a good time for them to learn. If you find you can't answer all their questions use the five-step process to find the answers.
- **Read in groups**. Developing a reading group is an excellent way to ensure you practice. Meet once a month or more often if you like. Make the purpose of the group twofold; firstly, discuss the contents of the book, articles or papers you read, and second, discuss the reading methods you used or had trouble with. Also, begin to explore other ways of reading effectively and bring that to the group. This way, group motivation will drive your learning forward. The more people you involve in your learning the easier it will be to stay motivated. It helps if there is someone there to help you along when you are having difficulties.
- **Learn something new every day**. No matter how small, learn something new. Keep a little book with your mini lesson of the day and you will be surprised how fast your general knowledge grows.

- **Learn a new word every day**. The better your
  vocabulary is the faster you will be able to read.
- **Be flexible**. If you find that your programme is too easy
  or too difficult, change it.
- **Don't stop after 21 days**. After your first 21 days you will
  have integrated the basics of speed-reading successfully.
  After that, take your reading to another level. You have
  already developed the habit of putting aside time to
  practice a new skill: keep that time available.

Below is a table to help you design your 21-day programme.

Day	Reading material	Time	What did I learn	New word
eg	The morning paper in 20 minutes or less. Purpose: practice five steps and gain information	20 min (0600–0620)	In this column write the most interesting thing you learnt	At least one new word and its definition
1				
2				
3				
4				
5				
6				
7				

8				
9				
10				
11				
12				
13				
14				
15				
16				
17				
18				
19				
20				
21				

Another useful tool is to keep a small notebook (together with your 21-day programme) to write down comments on the day's reading activities. What did you feel or think as you read? What was easy? What was difficult? What would you change about the way you read that day? What questions do you have?

A to Z of effective reading

A Active reading – Take notes, write in margins, circle, highlight, underline, think, argue, debate your way through whatever you read.

B Believe – You are capable of phenomenal things. Make this only your first step to effective reading. Look constantly for a better way of doing what you do.

C Concentration – Practice concentration techniques – remember that without concentration there is no memory, whether you are reading or remembering names.

D Determination – Frustration is a natural part of the learning process. Learn to enjoy it.

E Enjoy – The more you enjoy reading the less stressed you will be and the better you will remember what you read.

F **Flexibility** – Remember that you don't have to read fast all the time. Develop the skill of being able to identify when you can read fast and when you have to slow down.

G **Groups** – Sometimes a group of brains is better at staying motivated than one working alone.

H **Harassed** – If you are feeling stressed or tired your effectiveness will diminish. Stop and take a break especially if you feel you do not have the time.

I **Ideas** – Cross-reference, combine and elaborate on ideas between texts.

J **Justify** – Always ask yourself why you have to read it and what call it will have on your time.

K **Knowledge** – Make increasing your knowledge of yourself and the world around you a daily goal.

L **Learn** – Make it a habit to learn something new from your reading every day.

M **Manageable chunks** – Avoid reading for more than 30 minutes at a time.

N **Novels** – Using the five-step system for novels could spoil the ending. You will find, however, that the speed at which you can read novels will increase as a result of your speed-reading practice. You will not lose any of the enjoyment, in fact, you might find you finish more of the novels that you begin.

O **Organised** – Clear your desk of everything other than what you are working on at the time.

P **Purpose** – Have a clear and definite purpose whenever you read anything.

Q **Question** – Always ask questions. Just because what the author has said is in print, does not mean that he/she is right.

SATURDAY

R Revise – Refer to notes you have made previously whenever you have the opportunity to do so. Sometimes what we think at the time we only appreciate later.

S Stretch – Your body is involved in your reading as well as your mind. Reading can be a passive activity. When you read for any length of time your body might become stiff. Stretch whenever you take a break.

T Time – Take time to develop any new skill. Enjoy the gap between knowing you don't know how to do something and achieving success. Be patient with yourself.

U Use – The more you use the information you learn the better you will remember it and be able to apply it when you need it.

V Vocabulary – Use steps two and three (preview and passive reading) to identify words you don't understand. Look them up before you continue. If you encounter a word you don't understand while you are reading, take note, keep going and look it up at the end of the paragraph or section. You might find that the meaning becomes clear in the context of the text.

W Work is play with a suit on – Make whatever you do fun and you will be able to carry on longer and perform more effectively.

X X-plore – Find information from as many different sources as possible. Sometimes what you are looking for in a text you can get more quickly from a phonecall to an expert or a friend.

Y You – Reading and learning is a personal skill. Often you are the only one involved when you have to perform. Make sure that the techniques you use work for you. Try a variety of different ways of reading and learning and create a set of tools that suit you.

Z ZZZ Sleep – Avoid reading and studying at the expense of a good night's sleep. Take breaks whenever you need them. Read something enlightening, but light, before you go to sleep and think of what it means to you.